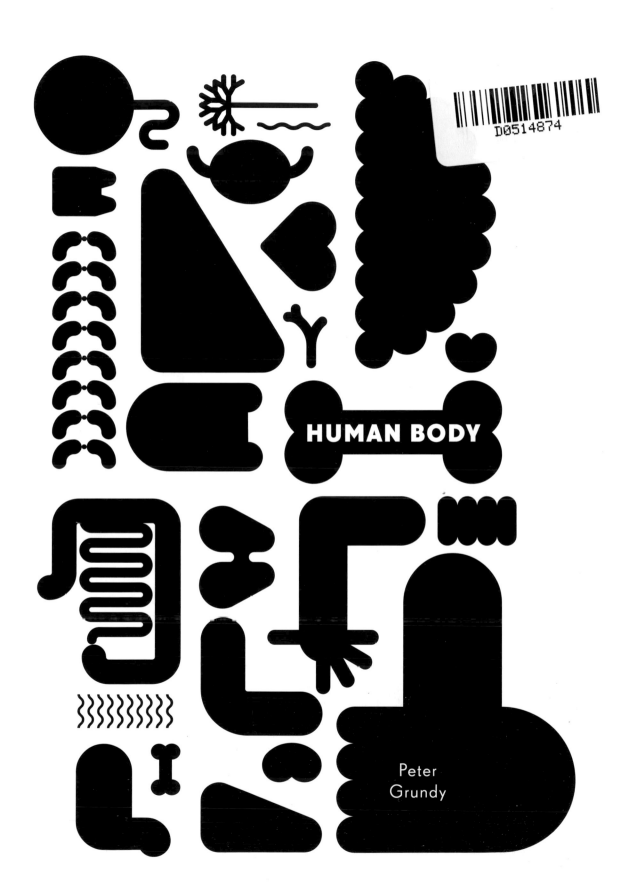

HUMAN BODY

Peter
Grundy

INTRODUCTION

The human body is an amazing feat of evolution. Its design is so complex and advanced that scientists are still discovering how parts of it work!

Your life began with just one tiny cell, which multiplied thousands of times over, becoming organized into tissues, organs, and other matter. When you become an adult, your body will contain more than 60 trillion cells.

Every day, your body does incredible things to keep you alive without you even having to think about it. This is thanks to systems that run automatically, such as your digestive system, which fuels you and provides you with energy, or your respiratory system, which provides you with oxygen.

What makes you even more amazing is your fantastic brain. It controls everything that happens in your body via your nervous system. It also allows you to think, talk, dream, remember, and imagine. Human intelligence has set us apart from animals for thousands of years, and it is still evolving and developing.

This book introduces you to some of the extraordinary things your body can do, brought to life by incredible infographics. So turn the page to understand the facts in the blink of an eye.

THE SENSES

Your senses keep you in touch with the world around you, making you aware of anything that might affect your body. They help you to avoid getting hurt by alerting you to dangers such as poisonous food or a hot flame, and bring you enjoyment in the form of beautiful sights and sounds, and delicious tastes and smells.

The five major senses are sight, hearing, touch, smell, and taste. In addition, you have other important sub-senses that help you to balance and walk, and feel pain and temperature.

All of your senses work in a similar way. Sensory organs, such as your eyes, have dedicated receptors. When these receptors detect a stimulus, such as a bright light, they send information via your nervous system to your spinal cord and brain, which process the information and help you to react in an appropriate way—in this case, blinking or shielding your eyes to protect them.

Your senses help you to make millions of these decisions every day, often completely subconsciously. Here is a closer look at the senses.

MAKING SENSE

· ·

What are the different senses,
and how do you perceive them?

Proprioception is possible thanks to sensory
receptors, which give you a sense of where the
various parts of your body are, allowing you to
concentrate on more than one thing at a time.

Without proprioception, drivers would be unable
to keep their eyes on the road while driving,
because they would need to pay attention to
the position of their arms and legs while working
the steering wheel and pedals.

PROPRIOCEPTION

Taste and **smell**
go together. Airborne
particles come through
your nasal passage and
enter your nose from the
back of the mouth.

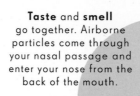

SMELL

HEARING

Your ears collect
sound waves,
which they turn
into vibrations.
Nerves then
transmit these
vibrations to your
brain to interpret
as **sound.**

Length of your ear
canal: 1 inch/
2.5 centimeters

When you are hungry,
you have a stronger
sense of **smell.**

You have 9,000 **taste**
buds on your tongue.

They are all
replaced every
few weeks.

TASTE

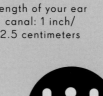
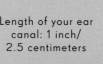

Unlike the other senses, your sense of touch can be found all over your body, thanks to nerve endings that discern texture and temperature, and sense pain and pressure.

The thermal **pain** threshold for humans is 113°F/45°C—under half the boiling point for water.

TEMPERATURE

Pain is important because it alerts you that your body is being harmed in some way.

TOUCH

You feel with your skin, tongue, throat, and hair.

PAIN

SIGHT

When you see, you can decipher three things: color, depth, and form.

Light rays enter your pupil and are converted into images in the retina. The optic nerve sends these images to your brain to be processed.

Average time between blinks: 2.8 seconds

Average duration of a single blink: 0.1–0.4 seconds

BALANCE

Your muscles, joints, eyes, and tiny hair cells in your inner ear transmit signals to your brain, which allows you to **balance** and, therefore, walk.

SIGHT

0.6 inch/
15 millimeters

SIZING UP

A baby's eyeball is 0.6 inches/15 millimeters in diameter. At age seven or eight, your eyeball reaches 1 inch/25 millimeters in diameter and stays that way for the rest of your life.

1 inch/
25 millimeters

SEEING THE BIG PICTURE

Your pupil takes in light rays. The iris (the colored ring around your pupil) controls how much light passes through by shrinking and enlarging the pupil.

The lens behind your pupil focuses the image onto the retina at the back of your eyeball.

The retina then passes the image to the brain via the optic nerve to be processed.

ON THE BLINK

By age sixty, your eyes begin to have:

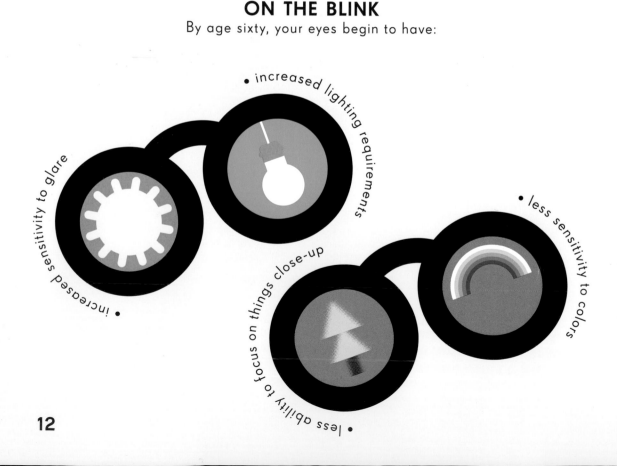

• increased lighting requirements

• increased sensitivity to glare

• less sensitivity to colors

• less ability to focus on things close-up

HUMAN VS. DOG

I SPY

A pattern that a dog can barely recognize at 20 feet/6 meters is large enough for a person with normal vision to identify at a distance of 75 feet/23 meters.

Humans have better depth perception because they evolved from apes, who needed to see branches clearly as they swung from tree to tree.

TOP DOG

Dogs cannot see color in the way that humans can. They are green-red color-blind. The spectrum of colors that they can see is close to the colors below.

However, dogs have better night vision and are good at seeing moving objects. This is because they evolved to hunt at night.

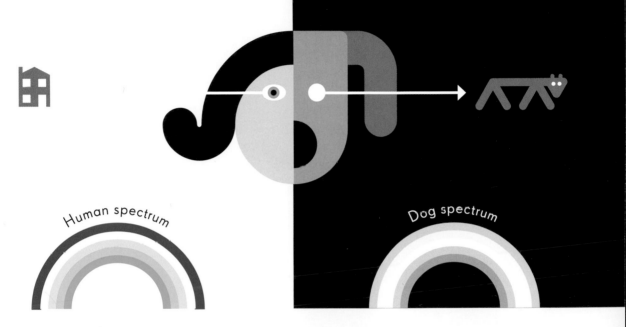

Human spectrum

Dog spectrum

INSECT VS. HUMAN

200 images per second

24 images per second

BUG EYES

Unlike humans, insects have compound eyes, made up of many separate units, meaning they view the world as a mosaic.

Insects can see far more images per second, making them difficult to swat because they can easily see you coming.

SEE YOU AROUND

Human eyes are front-facing, while a housefly has 360-degree vision to spot predators from any direction.

Insects cannot shift their visual focus to adjust it for distances, and so they see shapes badly.

TOUCH

HIT A NERVE

This illustration shows which parts of your body are the most sensitive. The bigger the body part is drawn, the more nerve endings you have there.

TOUCHY SUBJECT

Your sense of touch is important for feeling temperature, pain, and pressure. This prevents you from hurting yourself.

HOW ARE YOU FEELING?

MAGIC TOUCH

When you touch something, the sensation is picked up as signals by a network of nerves called neurons. They transmit signals via nerve receptors to the central nervous system. These are then analyzed by the brain.

14

HEARING

HOW LOUD?

Sound is measured in decibels (dB). Most humans have an auditory pain threshold of 130 decibels.

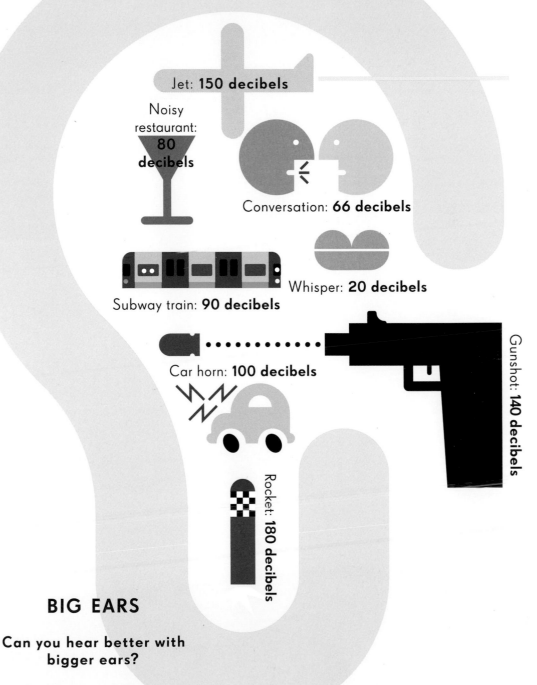

Jet: **150 decibels**

Noisy restaurant: **80 decibels**

Conversation: **66 decibels**

Whisper: **20 decibels**

Subway train: **90 decibels**

Car horn: **100 decibels**

Gunshot: **140 decibels**

Rocket: **180 decibels**

BIG EARS

Can you hear better with bigger ears?

Not really. Bigger ears can capture more sound waves, but the brain has a limit to the information it can process.

TASTE

GOOD TASTE

There are five main tastes:

Salty

Sweet

Bitter

Sour

Umami

*One micron is one thousandth of a millimeter.

TASTE-BUD TRIVIA

Total number of taste buds in your mouth (tongue, palate, cheeks)	10,000
Tongue	9,000
Height of taste bud	50–60 microns*
Diameter of taste bud	30–60 microns*
Number of receptors on each taste bud	50–150

TASTE TEST

Seventy-five percent of the flavors you taste come from what you smell. When you have a cold, much less air can travel through your nose, so you can't taste food in the same way because the odor molecules cannot reach the receptors.

SMELL

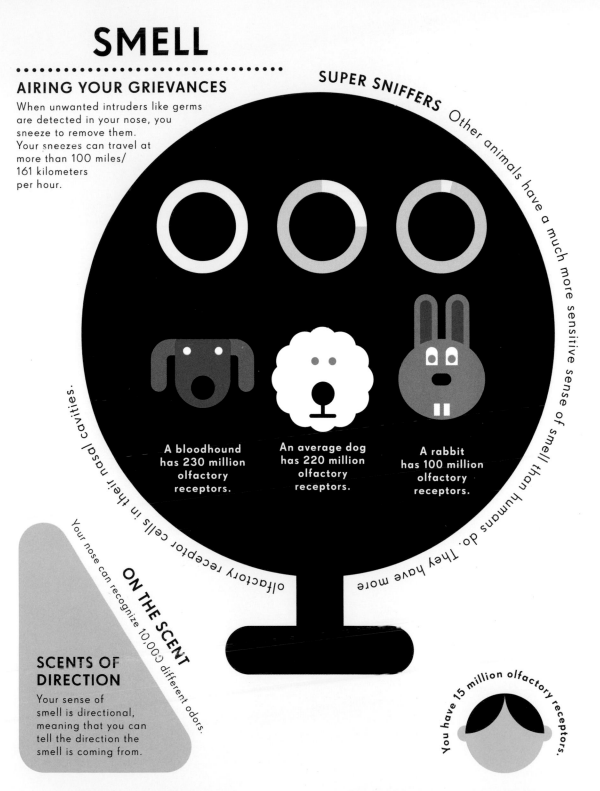

AIRING YOUR GRIEVANCES

When unwanted intruders like germs are detected in your nose, you sneeze to remove them. Your sneezes can travel at more than 100 miles/ 161 kilometers per hour.

SUPER SNIFFERS

Other animals have a much more sensitive sense of smell than humans do. They have more olfactory receptor cells in their nasal cavities.

A bloodhound has 230 million olfactory receptors.

An average dog has 220 million olfactory receptors.

A rabbit has 100 million olfactory receptors.

ON THE SCENT

Your nose can recognize 10,000 different odors.

SCENTS OF DIRECTION

Your sense of smell is directional, meaning that you can tell the direction the smell is coming from.

You have 15 million olfactory receptors.

GETTING UP YOUR NOSE

When molecules in the air enter your nose, they stimulate your smell receptors. These send a signal along the olfactory nerve to the olfactory bulb in your brain.

SOMETHING SMELLS FISHY

Your sense of smell warns you of dangers such as predators, poisonous food, or burning buildings. It can also help you to hunt out useful things like a healthy mate or a tasty meal.

REPRODUCTION

Every living thing needs to reproduce. For human beings, the process occurs when microscopic cells from a male and a female are combined. Male sex organs produce sperm, and female sex organs produce eggs. When male sperm enter the female womb, an egg, or ovum, can be fertilized and begin to grow.

This fertilized egg, or embryo, multiplies quickly as it develops from a single cell into a newborn baby that has more than five trillion cells. This process all happens in the span of just nine months!

Pregnancy is demanding on expectant mothers, who have to sleep and eat more in order to provide the developing fetus with everything it needs.

Once born, a baby continues to grow and requires constant care and attention. It lets its parents know if it needs anything by crying — loudly!

Although you might not remember it, this is the way each one of us started out! Here's a closer look at the journey from embryo to infant.

REPRODUCTION

MAN

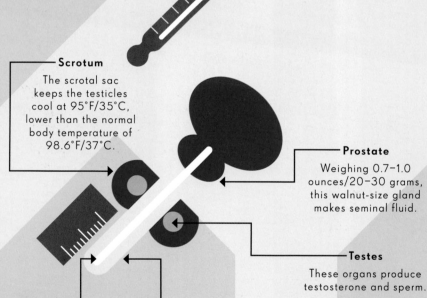

Scrotum
The scrotal sac keeps the testicles cool at 95°F/35°C, lower than the normal body temperature of 98.6°F/37°C.

Prostate
Weighing 0.7–1.0 ounces/20–30 grams, this walnut-size gland makes seminal fluid.

Testes
These organs produce testosterone and sperm.

Urethra
Both semen (containing sperm) and urine travel through this duct, but never at the same time!

Penis
This organ is made of a spongy tissue that can expand and contract.

The human penis, compared to its body size, is bigger than that of almost any other animal.

Every day the average male produces up to 85 million sperm per testicle!

WOMAN

Fallopian tube
The width of a piece of spaghetti, this tube helps the egg travel to the uterus.

Ovary
At birth, a baby girl has approximately 500,000 eggs in each ovary. Beginning at puberty, one egg is released every month.

Vagina
This passageway is 3–5 inches/ 8–10 centimeters long. The sperm swim up it towards the egg and a baby travels down it during childbirth.

Uterus
The fetus develops in the uterus, which contains some of the strongest muscles in the female body.

Umbilical cord
Connecting the fetus to the placenta, this tube stores 2 pounds/907 grams of protein by the time the baby is born—the same as 150 chicken eggs!

Cervix
To allow the baby to pass through it, the cervix grows 2.5 times in size during childbirth.

Clitoris
There are 8,000 nerve endings in the clitoris.

Placenta
This organ provides oxygen and nourishment to the baby, including up to 7.5 pints/3.5 liters of water a day.

Stem cells
These can grow into many different types of cells. They can be taken from the blood of the umbilical cord and used in bone-marrow transplants to help sick people.

Fetus
The unborn baby grows for approximately 9 months.

21

CONCEPTION

Rat
14 hours

Mouse
6 hours

Cow
28–50 hours

Sheep
30–48 hours

Human
24–48 hours

Bat
135 hours

SINK OR SWIM
How long do sperm live once inside the female?

SIZING UP
How does a sperm compare to an egg in size?

0.0002 inch/
0.005 mm

0.008 inch/
0.2 mm

If the sperm were the size of a man, the egg would be the size of a church.

STRONGEST SWIMMER
The successful sperm is one of how many?

Average number of sperm per ejaculation

Pig:
8,000
million

Human:
280
million

Rat:
58
million

There are more human sperm fighting for one egg than there are people in Indonesia, the world's fourth most populous country.

SPERM SPEED
How fast does a sperm travel?

Sperm are ejaculated at speeds of up to 30 mph/48.2 kph, after which the average sperm swims at 8 inches/20 cm per hour or 0.63 mph/1.01 kph.

It takes up to 68 minutes for a single sperm to reach an egg.

HOW DOES A SPERM'S EJACULATION SPEED COMPARE WITH OTHER TRAVEL SPEEDS?

		MPH	KPH
Butterfly		5	8
American woodcock		5	8
Single-hulled sailboat		21	33.8
Fastest human		23	37
Blue shark		24.5	39.4
Penguin		25	40.2
Gull		28	45
Sperm ejaculated		30	48.2
Killer whale		30	48.2
Swordfish		50	80.5

PREGNANCY

DISH IT OUT

During pregnancy, an expectant mother can crave unusual things. But what do these different food cravings mean?

CHOCOLATE
Extra magnesium is needed.
Magnesium helps to build and repair the body's tissues.

RED MEAT
Extra protein is needed.
The amino acids that make up protein are the building blocks of the body's cells.

ICE
Extra iron is needed.
Iron helps the body's immune system and is needed to produce blood.

CIGARETTE BUTTS
Smoking is harmful, especially during pregnancy.
Craving non-edible items is a condition known as pica. A craving for cigarette butts is connected with iron deficiency.

CELL SIZE

10,000
human cells could fit on
the head of a pin.

The average human cell measures 0.00003 inches/0.00076 mm

9,394,736,842
human cells could fit on
a soccer field.

EMBRYO FORMS

1 cell

EMBRYO DAY 5

100 cells

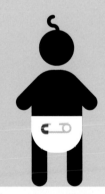

NEWBORN BABY

5 trillion cells

ADULT

60–90 trillion cells

BIRTH

The world population in 1950 was approximately **2.5 billion.**

The world population in 1850 was approximately **1.2 billion.**

The world population in 1650 was approximately **500 million.**

The world population in 1 AD was approximately **200 million.**

DOUBLE TROUBLE

Twins are on the rise!
In 1980 in the United States, one in every 53 babies born was a twin.
In 2009 in the United States, one in every 30 babies born was a twin.

ONE BORN EVERY MINUTE

The world population in 2011 was **6.9 billion.**

The total number of people that have ever lived on Earth is **108 billion.**

DAY BY DAY

Tuesday	13,336
Wednesday	13,034
Thursday	12,765
Friday	12,364
Monday	12,087
Saturday	8,308
Sunday	7,298

Average births per day in the United States, 2009.

Tuesdays have more births than any other day.

TIME'S UP

5% of babies are born on their actual due date.

10% of first-time pregnancies continue until two weeks past.

80% of babies are born between two weeks before and two weeks after their due date.

27

CRYBABY

WHAT DOES A BABY'S CRY MEAN?

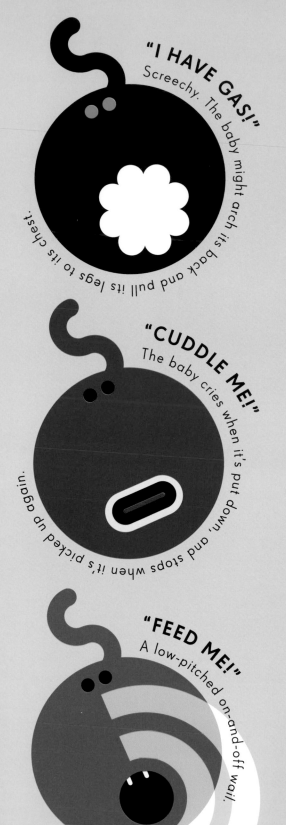

"I HAVE GAS!"
Screechy. The baby might arch its back and pull its legs to its chest.

"I'M TIRED!"
Starts with a whimper and builds to a wail.

"CUDDLE ME!"
The baby cries when it's put down, and stops when it's picked up again.

"OUCH!"
A sudden high-pitched shriek followed by loud wail.

"FEED ME!"
A low-pitched on-and-off wail.

SLEEPYHEAD

HOW MUCH SLEEP DOES
A GROWING CHILD NEED?

Age	Hours per day (approximately)
1–4 weeks	15–16
1–12 months	14–15
1–3 years	12–14
3–6 years	10–12
7–12 years	10–11
12–18 years	8–9

GROWING UP

HOW LONG DO PARTS OF THE
BODY TAKE TO FINISH GROWING?

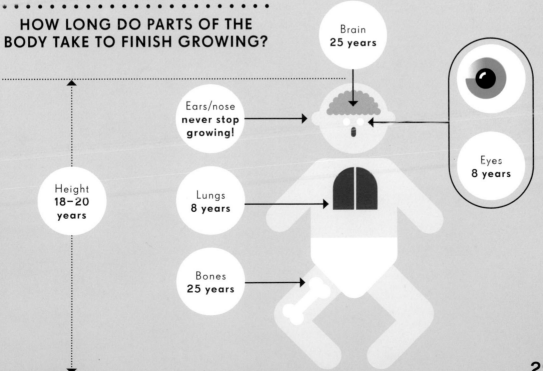

Brain
25 years

Ears/nose
**never stop
growing!**

Eyes
8 years

Height
18–20
years

Lungs
8 years

Bones
25 years

29

THE HEART

Although you might not think of it as a muscle, your heart is exactly that. In fact, it's one of the most durable muscles in your body, working day and night to keep you alive!

It is situated just left of center in your chest and supplies blood to the rest of your body via a complicated system of veins, arteries, and capillaries, which together with your heart make up your circulatory system.

Beating around the clock, your heart transports your blood to your lungs, where it picks up oxygen. Along with other vital nutrients, the blood delivers this oxygen to the rest of your body. Your heart responds to the rate at which your body uses up these resources by beating faster if you are exercising and slowing down if you are asleep.

Here's an introduction to why your heart is at the center of everything you do, and how to save it from skipping a beat.

HEART TO HEART

The heart is one of your most important organs. It pumps blood around your body.

RUSH OF BLOOD

1

Your heart is made up of four chambers, which fill with blood.

IN AND OUT

2

Four valves control the flow of blood in and out of your heart.

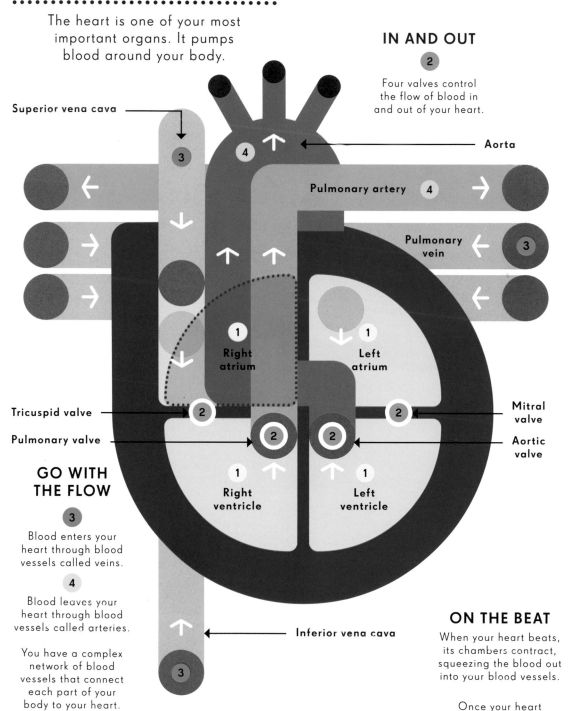

Superior vena cava

Aorta

Pulmonary artery

Pulmonary vein

Right atrium

Left atrium

Tricuspid valve

Mitral valve

Pulmonary valve

Aortic valve

Right ventricle

Left ventricle

Inferior vena cava

GO WITH THE FLOW

3

Blood enters your heart through blood vessels called veins.

4

Blood leaves your heart through blood vessels called arteries.

You have a complex network of blood vessels that connect each part of your body to your heart.

This is how your blood circulates through your body.

ON THE BEAT

When your heart beats, its chambers contract, squeezing the blood out into your blood vessels.

Once your heart relaxes, the chambers get bigger again and fill back up with blood.

HEART OF THE MATTER

HEART IN YOUR HANDS

Your heart is about the same size as your clenched fist.

WELL CONNECTED

Your heart is connected to veins, arteries, and millions of tiny blood vessels called capillaries, which deliver oxygen and nutrients to your cells.

COVERING GROUND

All the capillaries in the average adult's body form a huge network that, if spread out flat, would cover up to 10,764 square feet/ 1,000 square meters — an area greater than the size of three tennis courts.

ONE AT A TIME

Many of your capillaries are so tiny that only one blood cell can move through them at a time.

HEAVY HEART

An adult female's heart weighs 8 ounces/ 227 grams. An adult male's weighs 12 ounces/340 grams.

Each day, your heart beats about 100,000 times.

LIONHEARTED

Your heart is extremely strong, tough, and durable. In a year, a healthy adult's heart beats more than 36 million times.

With every beat, the heart pumps blood around the extensive network of vessels in your cardiovascular system.

COMING UP FOR AIR

Your heart delivers blood to your lungs to pick up oxygen (becoming oxygenated), and then sends it around the rest of your body. As your blood is circulated, it delivers oxygen to your organs, becoming deoxygenated until it returns to your lungs again.

Your body contains about 10.6 pints/5 liters of blood, which your heart is continuously circulating. This is enough blood to fill more than eight 20-ounce/0.6-liter bottles.

It pumps out 2.5 ounces/71 grams of blood with every heartbeat.

3 minutes

SPEED OF BLOOD

When you are at rest, your blood flows at 29 inches/73.7 centimeters per second in the middle cerebral artery (which feeds blood to your brain). That's 1.64 miles/2.6 kilometers per hour.

After three minutes of hyperventilating (breathing fast), the blood flow in this same artery decreases to almost half the speed.

JUMBO JOB

In a seventy-year lifetime, a heart beats over 2,500,000,000 times, pumping about 40,000,000 gallons/ 126,566,473 liters of blood.

That is enough blood to fill the fuel tanks of ten Boeing 747 jumbo jets every year.

35

FIGHTING FIT

Your heart is a muscle.
Like all muscles, when you exercise,
it gets bigger and stronger.

BEAT IT

95%

95% of normal adults have
a resting heart rate between
60 and 100 beats per minute.

SET YOUR HEART RACING

The stronger your heart,
the more blood it can pump
with every beat, meaning it
can cope with more strenuous
exercise with less strain.

A person who exercises regularly
has a stronger heart, which expels
more blood per beat. This results in
a lower resting heart rate.

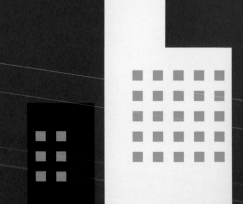

HEALTHY HEARTS
Here are six tips for
keeping a healthy heart:

Exercise

Eat well

Check your
blood pressure

Don't smoke

Watch
your weight

Limit alcohol
consumption

LITTLE TICKERS

The fetal heartbeat can be heard with a stethoscope beginning at twenty to twenty-two weeks.

GROW TOGETHER

An infant's heart and hands are the same size and grow at the same rate.

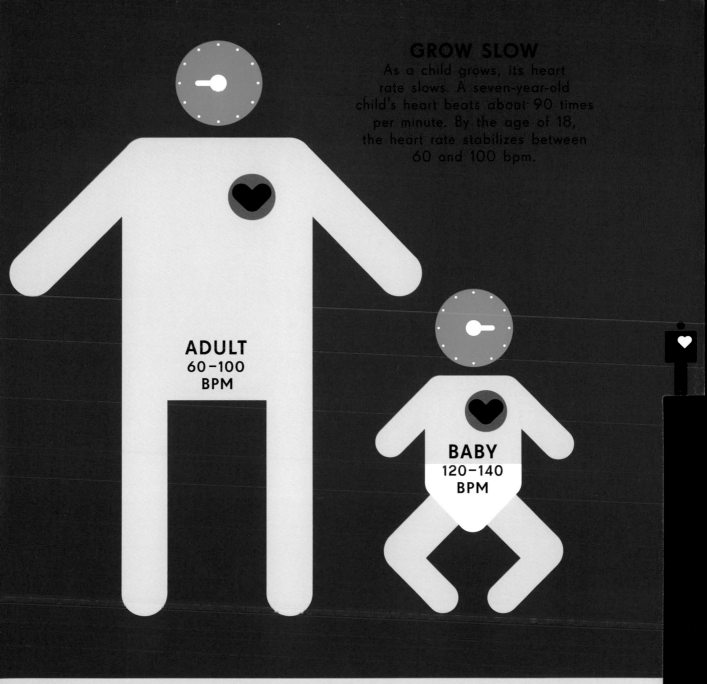

GROW SLOW

As a child grows, its heart rate slows. A seven-year-old child's heart beats about 90 times per minute. By the age of 18, the heart rate stabilizes between 60 and 100 bpm.

ADULT
60–100
BPM

BABY
120–140
BPM

KEEPING TIME

The heart begins to develop in week five of pregnancy and keeps growing throughout.

THE BRAIN

The brain is at the center of your nervous system, and is what makes you *you*! Without your brain you wouldn't be able to think, learn, create, or feel emotions.

At the same time that you are busy doing these things, your brain is also subconsciously making sure that your eyes keep blinking, your lungs keep breathing, and your heart keeps beating. In fact, it's in charge of pretty much everything in your body.

Your nervous system relays messages between your brain and the rest of your body, shuttling sensory information and instructions back and forth at lightning speed.

Your brain is so complicated that scientists are still figuring out exactly what it is capable of and how it works. James D. Watson described the human brain as "the most complex thing we have yet discovered in our universe."

BRAIN BOX

Your brain has many different parts, each of which controls different things. Here are some of the most important parts of your brain.

SKULL
1

Your brain is protected by your skull, which is made up of twenty-one bones that have fused together, plus the mandible.

CEREBRAL CORTEX
2

Among other things, this helps you to remember, make sense of your surroundings, think, and speak.

ANTERIOR CINGULATE GYRUS
3

This looks after your blood pressure and heart rate, and plays a part in controlling your emotions.

THALAMUS
4

This controls all of your senses.

PARIETAL LOBE
5

This helps you to make sense of numbers, words, and maps.

HYPOTHALAMUS
6

This controls a variety of things, including your body's temperature, hunger, thirst, and sleepiness.

FRONTAL LOBE
7

This is associated with your character and personality. It also helps you to identify differences and make decisions.

OLFACTORY BULB
8

This processes the information that your nose sends to your brain, giving you your sense of smell.

HIPPOCAMPUS
10

This is where your memory lives.

BRAIN STEM
12

Messages between your body and your brain travel through your brain stem. It makes sure that your heart, lungs, and other organs keep working without you having to think about it.

CEREBROSPINAL FLUID
9

Your brain floats in cerebrospinal fluid within your skull, which keeps out infections and cushions it against impact.

CEREBELLUM
11

This helps you to keep your balance and coordinate movement.

QUICK THINKING

If a bee lands on your foot, sensory neurons in your skin send this information through your spinal cord to your brain at a speed of more than 150 mph/241 kph.

Your brain then uses motor neurons to transmit the message back through your spinal cord to your foot to shake the bee off quickly. Motor neurons can relay this information at more than 200 miles/322 kilometers per hour.

AIR HEAD

Gray matter uses 94 percent of the oxygen that travels to your brain.

HEAD SPACE

Gray matter fills up about 40 percent of your brain.

GRAY AREA

Gray matter is the part of your brain controlled by nerve endings all over your body. You use it for:

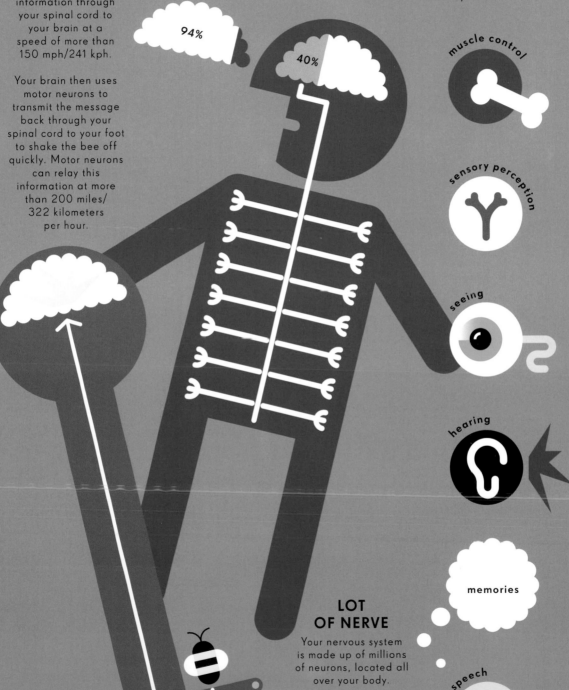

94%

40%

muscle control

sensory perception

seeing

hearing

memories

speech

LOT OF NERVE

Your nervous system is made up of millions of neurons, located all over your body.

Your nerves relay messages between your body and your brain through your spinal column.

ALL IN THE MIND

Your mind is not actually a physical part of your body. It is your conceptual way of understanding things and is what makes you unique. It allows you to think independently from others and makes you aware of everything that is going on around you. Your mind has four different functions:

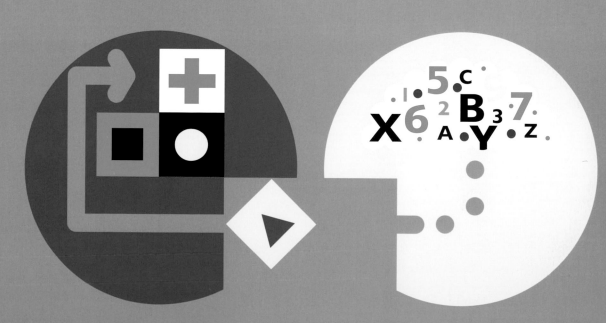

THOUGHT

Helps you to make sense of the world through problem-solving, reasoning, and decision-making.

MEMORY

This is your ability to store and later remember information, knowledge, or experiences—your own personal library.

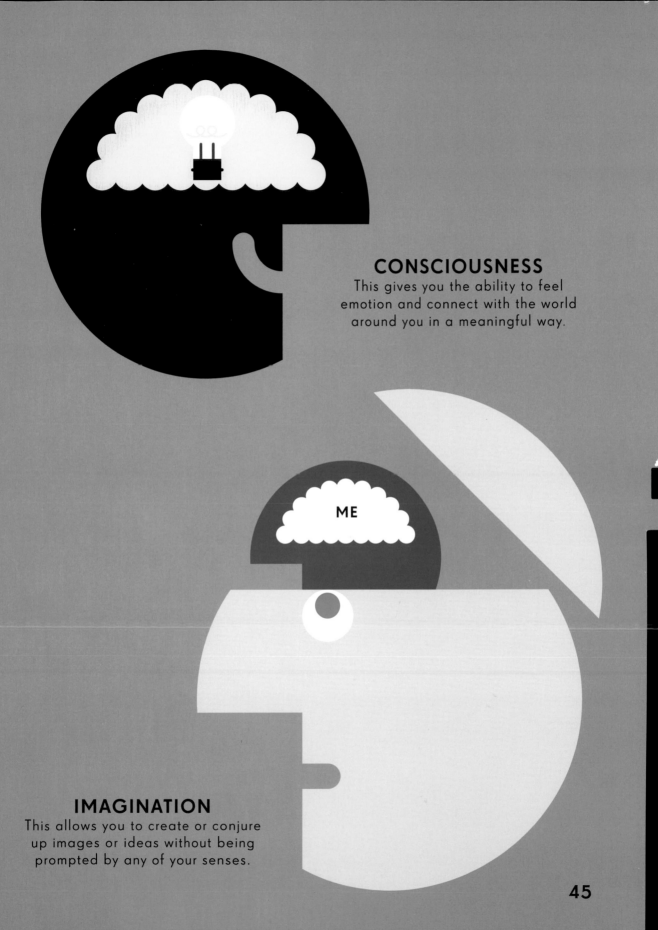

CONSCIOUSNESS

This gives you the ability to feel emotion and connect with the world around you in a meaningful way.

ME

IMAGINATION

This allows you to create or conjure up images or ideas without being prompted by any of your senses.

45

THINKING BIG

· · · · · · · · · · · · · ·

BABY-BRAINED
You can first see the human brain developing in an unborn baby at around sixteen days.

MAKING SENSE
The sense of touch is the first to develop. An unborn baby responds to touch on the lips and cheeks after eight weeks, and can feel other parts of its body after fourteen weeks.

Its sense of taste may develop by twelve weeks, and after twenty-two weeks it can start to hear, too.

AT THE READY
A newborn baby's brain contains more than 100 billion brain cells, called neurons. These are almost all the brain cells it will ever need.

SIZING UP

A baby's brain keeps growing after birth,
quickly increasing in size during the first two years.

A two-year-old's brain is about 80 percent
of the size of an adult's brain.

LIVE WIRE

As a child's brain develops, it
becomes a complex network of
synapses—connections that wire
together different parts of the
brain. The number of these synapses
grows quickly during early childhood.

LOST CONNECTION

A three-year-old has twice as
many synapses as an adult,
which helps them to quickly absorb
new information and form
memories. The synapses that are
not used repeatedly are lost.

POWER NAP

When you sleep, your body has the chance to grow and repair itself.

LOSING SLEEP

As you grow older, and the rate at which your body is developing slows down, your need for sleep decreases.

NEWBORNS
15–16 hours

24-HOUR CLOCK

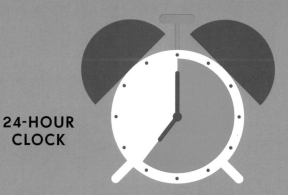

INFANTS
14–15 hours

TODDLERS
12 –14 hours

CHILDREN
10–11 hours

TEENAGERS
8.5–9.25 hours

ADULTS
7–9 hours

LOSE SLEEP

The most common emotion people have in dreams is anxiety. This may be due to activity in the part of the brain that deals with worry.

FORGET IT

You forget around 95% of your dreams. This may be because the part of your brain that stores memory isn't active while you are asleep.

BLACK OUT

Around 80% of people dream in color. Some people, however, dream in black-and-white. This may be because they watched black-and-white televisions when they were children.

IN YOUR DREAMS

Dreams occur during the rapid eye movement (REM) stage of sleep when the parts of your brain that are linked with imagination, creativity, and anxiety are active. This is is why they can be strange, exciting, and frightening.

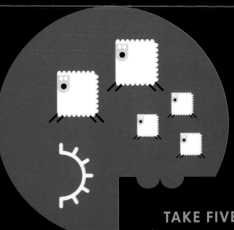

IN DEEP

When you sleep, your brain enters a subconscious state, making you less aware of your surroundings and allowing your body to rest.

TAKE FIVE

The average person has 3–5 dreams per night.

DIGESTION

We all enjoy a good meal, and eating is one of the most important parts of your day. Your digestive system is a complex machine that takes the food you eat and extracts energy and nutrients from it that your body can use.

You need this energy to do absolutely everything. Different foods provide different nutrients that keep you healthy, so it's important to eat a varied diet of many different food groups.

Although under-eating can lead to malnutrition, eating too much causes your body to store excess calories as fat, which can lead to obesity and other related health risks. This problem is on the rise in developed countries with plentiful food supplies. But if you eat well and have an active life, maintaining a healthy weight shouldn't be difficult.

Here's a guide to the inner workings of your gut, and some tips on eating right.

MOUTH TO FEED

Have you ever wondered what happens when you eat? Here's a closer look at your digestive system.

BREAKING BREAD

The food that you eat contains nutrients that enable your body to function properly. However, these nutrients can't be absorbed into the bloodstream and delivered around your body until they have been broken down into smaller molecules. It's your digestive system's job to do this, bit by bit.

MOUTH

Food enters your body through your mouth. Here the food is broken down, making it easy to pass through your digestive system.

EPIGLOTTIS/ PHARYNX

Food and liquids travel down your pharynx, or throat, into your esophagus, or gullet.

Your epiglottis, a flap of cartilage at the root of your tongue, prevents food from entering your windpipe.

STOMACH

Your stomach creates gastric juices—up to 3.2 pints/1.5 liters per day! This makes the food particles smaller and more soluble.

A pepsin enzyme in your stomach helps break down proteins. Any nasty bacteria in the food should be killed off by hydrochloric acid.

The inner surface of the stomach is lined by a mucus membrane known as the gastric mucosa.

SMALL INTESTINE

Your small intestine digests and absorbs fats, proteins, and carbohydrates. Your food may stay as long as four hours in the small intestine.

Cells in the small intestine's wall help neutralize the acid and make enzymes to digest the food. This digested food then enters the bloodstream.

LARGE INTESTINE

When food reaches your large intestine, your body has absorbed most of its nutrients, and all that is left of it is a watery substance.

Your large intestine absorbs most of the water and breaks down the undigested leftovers (mostly fiber) with bacteria, and turns it into feces, or poop.

TEETH

Your front teeth are designed for biting off small chunks of food, and your back teeth are rounded, to grind food into small, easy-to-swallow pieces.

SALIVARY GLANDS

These make saliva, which mixes with the food, making it easier to swallow and digest.

TONGUE

The taste buds on your tongue taste the food. Sometimes, bad tastes can mean the food contains dangerous bacteria.

ESOPHAGUS

Contractions squeeze the food down to your stomach. It takes about ten seconds for food to arrive after swallowing.

GALLBLADDER

Your gallbladder is a sac filled with bile, which helps fats to be absorbed into the bloodstream.

LIVER

Your liver produces bile. Nutrient-rich blood is filtered by your liver, which takes out waste and harmful substances.

RECTUM

Feces are kept here until ready to be released via your anus.

PANCREAS

Your pancreas makes digestive enzymes and releases insulin and glucagon into your bloodstream to control sugar levels.

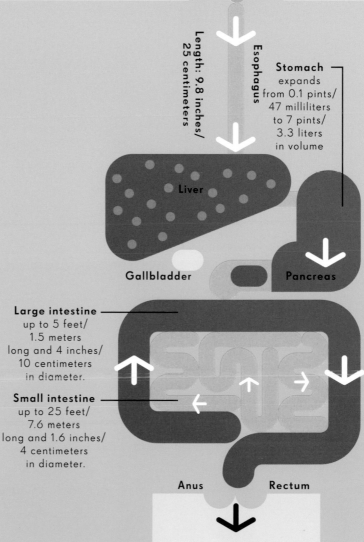

HUNGER PAINS

If you haven't eaten in a while, the levels of sugar in your blood can dip. When this happens, your body releases a hormone that tells your stomach muscles to contract, making you feel hungry.

Particularly strong and painful stomach contractions are known as hunger pangs.

FROM MOUTH TO SOUTH

Food takes between 24–36 hours to pass through the gastrointestinal tract.

Salivary glands

Teeth

Food

Mouth

Tongue

Epiglottis   Pharynx

Esophagus

Length: 9.8 inches/ 25 centimeters

Stomach expands from 0.1 pints/ 47 milliliters to 7 pints/ 3.3 liters in volume

Liver

Gallbladder

Pancreas

Large intestine up to 5 feet/ 1.5 meters long and 4 inches/ 10 centimeters in diameter.

Small intestine up to 25 feet/ 7.6 meters long and 1.6 inches/ 4 centimeters in diameter.

Anus   **Rectum**

NUTRITIOUS AND DELICIOUS

Eating good food isn't only enjoyable, it's key for staying healthy and energized.

Here are the different ways in which the food you eat fuels your body.

MACRONUTRIENTS

Carbohydrates, proteins, and fats are all macronutrients, and your body needs quite a lot of these to function properly.

They are in the healthy sugary, fatty, and starchy food and drinks that you consume, and they break down to provide your body with energy. Your body needs this energy to grow, repair itself, be active, and stay warm.

There are many less healthy sources of macronutrients available too, such as fast foods, which use processed ingredients and are often less nutritious than freshly prepared alternatives. Try to avoid including too much of this kind of food in your diet as it may lead to weight gain and bad health.

CRUCIAL CALORIES

You can count the energy that each type of food offers your body in calories. The number of calories you burn off in a day depends on how much energy you use.

Your body burns calories without you noticing. Keeping your heart beating, your lungs breathing, and all of your other organs functioning properly uses up energy.

On average, adult women burn around 2,000 calories per day, and adult men burn 2,500 calories.

Children, with smaller bodies to fuel, need fewer calories.

Athletes, who expend a lot of energy exercising vigorously, need more.

WEIGHING IT UP

Any calories that you eat but don't use are stored as fat. Having too many unused calories left over at the end of the day can lead to weight gain, but eating properly and staying active should keep you at a healthy weight without having to think about it at all.

GOING HUNGRY

If your body doesn't take in enough nutrients, you can become malnourished. While this is often linked to poverty and not consuming enough food, it can sometimes simply mean that your diet is lacking the necessary variety.

Malnutrition can lead to disease and illness, and it is a big problem in the world, affecting around one in twelve people.

MACRONUTRIENTS

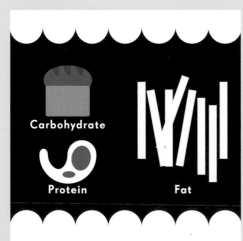

Carbohydrate

Protein

Fat

MICRONUTRIENTS

Vitamins
Minerals

MICRONUTRIENTS

Vitamins and minerals are micronutrients and, although your body needs them in relatively small amounts, they are essential for keeping you healthy.

To get enough of every vitamin and mineral, you need to eat a wide variety of foods, especially fruits, vegetables, grains, and beans.

MAGICAL MINERALS

The minerals in your body are the same ones that can be found in the earth, like iron, zinc, calcium, and copper. You need just a tiny amount of each one, but they are vital for helping your nerves, heart, hormones, immune system, and many other things.

VITAL VITAMINS

Some vitamins are water-soluble and pass through your body quickly. Others are fat-soluble and can be stored (especially around your liver) until you need them. Here are some ways in which vitamins are vitally important to your body.

VITAMIN A keeps your eyes sharp.

THE B VITAMINS help your energy levels.

VITAMIN C keeps your immune system strong.

VITAMIN D looks after your teeth and bones.

VITAMIN E helps your red blood cells.

VITAMIN K helps your blood to clot when it needs to form a scab.

OTHER ESSENTIALS

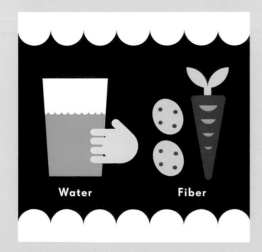

Water   Fiber

WONDROUS WATER

It's important that you consume enough water every day. There is more water in your body than anything else! On average, water makes up 60 percent of your body weight.

Of course, you can drink water from a glass, but it is also in some foods, particularly fruits and vegetables.

FABULOUS FIBER

Dietary fiber isn't nutritious and can't be broken down, but it is important for helping food pass through your digestive system.

It is present in cereals, brown bread, beans, lentils, fruits, and vegetables.

BETTER OUT THAN IN

Not everything you eat is useful or good for you, so your body has developed ways for food to make a quick exit.

POOPED OUT

You expel from your anus anything that your body hasn't absorbed or stored during the process of digestion. As we've discovered, what comes out the other end is feces, or poop.

Your poop is made of 75 percent water and 25 percent solid matter.

This solid matter is made up of dead bacteria, indigestible food matter, cholesterol and other fats, inorganic substances (such as calcium phosphate), and protein.

THE BRISTOL STOOL CHART

Doctors use this chart to work out how healthy you are by looking at your feces.

BROWNING GLORY

The perfect poop is sausage-shaped with cracks, or smooth and soft, as they are easy to pass. They should not contain any excess water.

STUMBLING BLOCK

Nutty and lumpy sausage-shapes may mean that you are constipated and that food isn't passing through your digestive tract fast enough.

MUDDY WATERS

Soft blobs and mushy or watery poops tend toward diarrhea, meaning that food is passing through your digestive system too fast for your body to absorb nutrients.

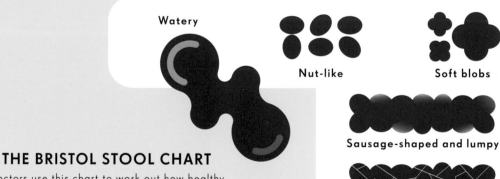

Watery

Nut-like

Soft blobs

Sausage-shaped and lumpy

Sausage-shaped with cracks

Smooth and soft

Mushy

CLEANED OUT

Your kidneys clean your blood and process urine to rid your body of excess water, salt, and other waste substances.

GAGGING TO GO

Vomiting is your body's way of forcing out anything that has upset your stomach.

Although it is unpleasant, vomiting via your mouth means that harmful substances don't travel through the rest of your digestive tract, where they could cause more problems.

TESTING THE WATERS

Urine is around 95 percent water, depending on how much you drink and how much you sweat.

TOPPING UP

When you are sick, your body loses fluids, salts, and minerals. So it is crucial that you drink enough water and eat something to replace the lost nutrients.

FULL TANK

An average adult urinates up to 3.5 pints/2 liters per day, which would fill 385 bathtubs* in an average lifetime.

FANG-TASTIC

Before you vomit, your mouth automatically fills with saliva to protect your teeth from the acid coming up from your stomach.

*Each illustration represents 55 bathtubs.

WEIGHTY MATTER

· ·

Having a certain amount of body fat is important for your health. If you are active and eat good food in reasonable portions, your weight should stay at a healthy level.

However, around the world, we are eating more and exercising less, meaning that obesity (being dangerously overweight) is on the rise.

Here are some of the facts surrounding this weighty matter.

WHO?
Who is considered to be clinically obese?

A person is classified as clinically obese when their body mass index (BMI) is in the 95th percentile. This is calculated by offsetting a person's weight against his or her height, which indicates whether or not that person is healthy.

WHAT?
What's the problem with being obese?

Although carrying a little extra weight isn't dangerous, being clinically obese puts a strain on your body and can lead to a number of health risks, including diabetes, heart problems, and even cancer.

WHEN?
When do you become obese?

If you eat more calories than you can burn off in a day, the unused calories are turned into fat. If you continue to take on more calories than you need, your body stores more and more fat over time. Being obese means that your body is carrying an unhealthy amount of this fat.

WHERE?
Where is obesity a problem?

Obesity is becoming especially common in the West, affecting around one in four adults in the U.K.

WHY?
Why are we getting fatter?

Increasingly inactive lifestyles and cheap, sugary, and fatty foods are increasing obesity rates.

SWEET TOOTH

Years ago, humans were more active and had to work a lot harder to find and hunt for food. Because they needed the energy, they developed a taste for foods high in calories, like sugary and fatty foods.

EYES BIGGER THAN YOUR STOMACH

We have inherited this same built-in taste for sugary and fatty foods, but now our lifestyles are much less active.

LARGER THAN LIFE

The unused calories that we consume turn to fat, meaning that people around the world are getting fatter than they used to be.

Calories

Fat

Although around 13 percent of the world's population is living in hunger . . .

a greater percent of people in the world die from problems connected with obesity.

THE SKELETON

Your body is supported by your skeleton, an interconnecting structure of 206 bones. These work together with your muscles, joints, tendons, and ligaments to form your musculoskeletal system, which allows you to move, balance, push, and lift.

Your muscles and bones have other crucial roles, too. Your bones provide protection for vital organs such as the heart and lungs, manufacture blood cells, and store minerals until your body needs them.

Your muscles keep your body warm, your heart beating, your eyes in focus, and your digestive system functioning.

This complex system is a work of art that has been developing over thousands of years, adapting gradually as humans learned to stand and walk on two legs rather than four.

Here's the inside story on how your bones and muscles keep you on your toes.

THE HUMAN SKELETON

There are 206 bones in your body that make up your skeleton. Every bone has a job: some provide protection to your organs, while others make it possible to move.

EAR

Your ears contain the smallest bones in your body, the stirrups in each middle ear. They are part of the system that carries sound signals to the brain. They are just 0.12 inches/3 millimeters long—the size of a grain of rice.

FACE

Your face is made up of fourteen bones, including your mandible, or jawbone. Your jawbone is the hardest bone in your body.

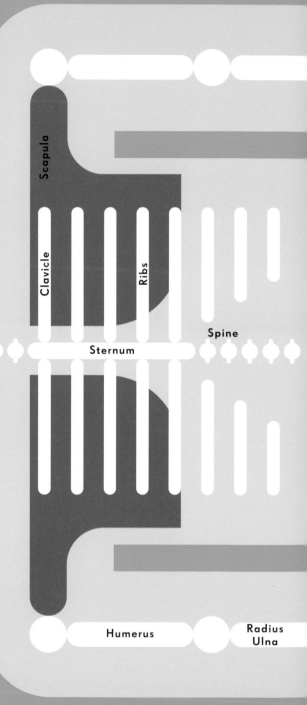

Scapula

Clavicle

Ribs

Spine

Cranium

Mandible

Sternum

Humerus

Radius
Ulna

SKULL

Your skull is made up of two sets of bones: your face at the front of your head and cranium at the back. Your cranium protects your brain and is made up of eight flat bones.

There are twenty-two bones in your skull altogether. A baby's skull hasn't fused together, (which makes it easier for the baby to be born). These plates fuse after two years to form an adult skull.

SHOULDER

Two bones form your shoulder: the collarbone (clavicle) and the shoulder blade (scapula). The two bones together form the structure from which your arm hangs.

The collarbone is the only bone that joins directly to the rib cage.

SPINE

Your spine is made up from a column of thirty-three bones called vertebrae, which protect your spinal cord and help you stand upright.

PELVIS

Your pelvis is joined to your spine at the sacrum, a bone made up of five fused vertebrae in the lower part of the spine.

A woman's pelvis is shallower and wider than a man's, making it possible for a baby to pass through when she gives birth.

LEGS

The bones in your legs are the longest in your body. Your patellas (kneecaps) float in front of your knee joints, protecting the ends of the bones that meet there. At birth, babies don't have kneecaps. Instead they have an undeveloped bit of cartilage, which make their legs more flexible.

Femur   Patella   Tibia   Metatarsals   Phalanges   Tarsals

Sacrum
Coccyx

COCCYX

You've inherited your coccyx from your primate ancestors. This is the remnants of your tailbone!

RIBS

Your ribs act like a cage to protect your vital organs, including your lungs and your heart.

FEET

You have twenty-six bones in each foot. These give your feet the flexibility to walk.

Pelvis

Metacarpals

Phalanges

Carpals

ARMS

Your upper and lower arms are joined at your elbow by a joint that connects your humerus and your radius and ulna, which allows you to rotate your hand and forearm by more than 180 degrees.

HANDS

You have twenty-seven bones in each hand, with three phalanges in each of your fingers and two in your thumb. These attach to five metacarpals in your hand, which connect to the carpal bones in your wrist.

HANDS & FEET

More than half of the bones in your body are in your hands and feet and they are both based on the same design.

JOINTS

Without joints, you would be a bit . . . stuck! Not only would you not be able to move, but your body wouldn't have the flexibility to grow. Here's a closer look at what your joints have to offer.

GROWTH

Although you can't move them, you have joints in your skull. These allow your brain to grow. You also have joints in places like your knee to allow your legs to grow longer.

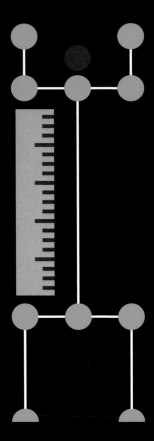

MOVEMENT

Different types of joints allow your limbs to move in different ways. They range from hinge joints, such as those in your elbows, which allow you to bend in just one direction, to ball-and-socket joints, such as those in your shoulders, which let you move your arms in all directions.

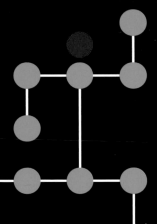

STABILITY

Ligaments around your joints keep you from making movements that are too big and would be harmful to your body.

SUPPORT

Joints connect your bones, offering support to your body and giving you structure so that you're not unstable like a jellyfish!

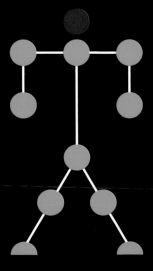

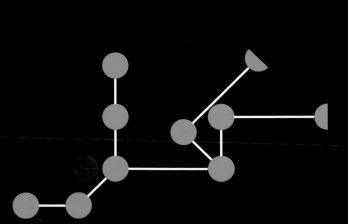

JOINTS

There are three kinds of joints in your body, each one named after the material that unites the bones together.

ON THE HOP

Movement in your limbs is possible thanks to your **synovial joints.** These joints are surrounded by a sac of synovial fluid, which cushions impact between the bones forming the joint. These are found in most of the major joints in your limbs, such as your elbow.

Synovial joints absorb impact, allowing you to do things like hop without damaging the bones in your hip. They also reduce friction, meaning that your femur doesn't grind against your pelvis when you walk.

Synovial joints

Fibrous joints

Cartilaginous joints

GOOD TO GROW

Fibrous joints connect bones using fibrous tissue. The plates in your skull are connected by fibrous joints called sutures. At birth, these joints have not fused together, which allow the skull to grow with the brain.

The connected parts grow stronger with age, and by the age of twenty, the sutures will have closed over, connecting your skull bones permanently.

LET SLIP

Sometimes the ends of your bones are covered by a layer of cartilage — a firm and slippery material. The vertebrae in your spine are connected by these **cartilaginous joints.**

Sometimes the cartilage in these joints becomes bone as you grow older. This happens with the cartilaginous joints in your knees.

BARE BONES

· · · · · · · · · · · · · · · ·

There's more to your bones than you might think: each one of your bones is made up from different layers.

COMPACT BONE

Compact (or cortical) bone is the hard outer part of the bone. It is extremely tough, with little holes that allow blood vessels and nerves to pass through.

PERIOSTEUM

The outer part of your bone is covered in a membranous layer of nerves and blood vessels. These supply the bone with the nutrients it needs.

CANCELLOUS BONE

Inside your compact bone, a hollow, mesh-structured matter called cancellous (or spongy) bone can be found. It contains your bone marrow.

BONE MARROW

This flexible, jelly-like substance is found in the heads of long bones. It produces platelets and red and white blood cells — up to 500 billion per day!

HARD WORKER

· ·

Your skeleton has six major jobs.

Support

MOVE A MUSCLE

Your joints, together with your muscles, allow you to move.

Movement

PILLAR OF SUPPORT

Your skeleton is your body's scaffolding, giving it shape.

BLOODY BUSINESS

Your blood cells are created in your bone marrow.

Production

Protection

SELF DEFENSE

Your skeleton protects your vital organs, such as your brain, your lungs, and heart.

ON THE LEVEL

Your bone cells work together with your kidneys and your gut to maintain a healthy level of calcium.

Storage

Regulation

KEPT IN STORAGE

Your bones store calcium, iron, and other minerals.

MUSCLE MAN

Your muscles are important to
your body for a number of reasons.

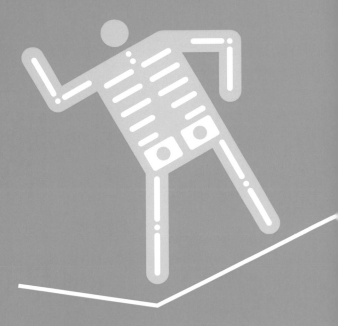

HEAT

As much as 70 percent
of your body heat
comes from your
muscles. Movement and
exercise raise your body
temperature, and when
you are cold, your
muscles shiver to keep
you warm.

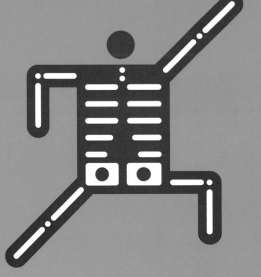

BALANCE

Keeping your balance
wouldn't be possible
without your muscles.
Signals from your inner
ear travel to your brain,
which processes the
information and sends
messages back via your
nervous system to
your muscles, stopping
you from toppling over.

MOVEMENT

Your skeletal
muscles allow you to
move. This includes
big movements, like
standing, walking
and lifting, and also
small ones, like making
facial expressions,
such as a smile or a
frown, or using your
mouth to talk.

STRENGTH

The more you work
your muscles, the
stronger they become.
This isn't only the case
with muscles you can
see, like the biceps in
your arms, but also
those that are hidden,
like your heart.

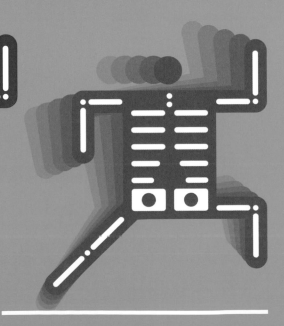

TRIPLE TALENT

You have more than six hundred muscles in your body, which fall into three different categories: skeletal, cardiac, and smooth.

SKELETAL MUSCLE

Your skeletal muscles are voluntary muscles, meaning that you are in charge of what they do. They are attached to your bones with tendons. As your muscles contract, they pull the tendons, which in turn move the bones.

CARDIAC MUSCLE

Your heart is made up of a special type of involuntary muscle, and from where it lies in your chest, it can pump blood all the way around your body. It changes its beat to make sure your body has just the right amount of oxygen by speeding up when you're running and slowing down when you are relaxed.

SMOOTH MUSCLE

Your smooth muscles are involuntary, meaning that you have no control over them. They are important for lots of things: helping to move food through your digestive system, focusing your eyes, controlling your bladder, or giving a woman's uterus contractions when she is in labor.

Heart

Stomach

Bladder

Eye

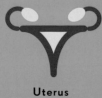

Uterus

WALKING TALL

BACK TO BASICS

All animals that have a backbone are called vertebrates. There are 64,000 different vertebrate species, including us human beings!

All vertebrate animals have a spine. What makes ours different?

SPINAL CORD

Your vertebrae are hollow and protect your spinal cord, which runs up through the middle.

SPINOUS PROCESS

This wing-like structure attaches to muscles and ligaments.

VERTEBRAL BODY

This is the largest part of a vertebra and is cylindrical in shape.

INTERVERTEBRAL DISC

This is a layer of cartilage that forms a cartilaginous joint between neighboring vertebrae.

COLUMN CLOSE-UP

BENDING THE RULES

As mankind took to walking, the human spine evolved into an S shape, allowing humans to transition from crawling on four legs to walking on two.

This S shape is called a lumbar bend, and it is this forward bend in your spine that allows you to stand upright.

TWIST AND SHOUT

Many people suffer from back problems due to the way our spines are designed.

Our style of walking, in which we swing our arms in step, twists our bodies side to side.

This can wear down the protective discs of cartilage and lead to back pain as the vertebrae rub against one another.

COCCYX

This is another large bone made of four vertebrae fused together.

It is sometimes called your tailbone, because your primate ancestor's tail would have been here.

When you sit back, it helps to support your body weight.

VERTEBRAL COLUMN

Your spinal column, or spine, is made up of thirty-three bones known as vertebrae.

CERVICAL VERTEBRAE

These are connected to your skull and support your head and neck.

A joint between your first and second vertebrae allows your head to pivot side to side.

THORACIC VERTEBRAE

These form the middle segment of your spinal cord.

They are connected to your ribs, making up part of your chest.

LUMBAR VERTEBRAE

This is the largest segment of your spinal column.

These vertebrae bear the weight of your body and allow you to move.

SACRUM

This large bone is made of five vertebrae that fuse together as you grow. This process finishes around age twenty-six.

HUMAN FACTORY

Your body is amazingly productive. It creates substances such as mucus and sweat to regulate your temperature and keep you well nourished, infection-free, and in good health.

These processes create some unpleasant by-products that you need to get rid of. These by-products can be in liquid, solid, or gaseous form, and your body has different ways of excreting each one—sometimes with comical sounds and smells!

The average human produces enormous quantities of these substances over the course of a lifetime. Thinking about different ways in which they could be used yields some surprising facts!

Warm and moist, your body also makes an attractive place for things like bacteria, viruses, and even parasites to live and reproduce. If you're squeamish, you might not want to look too closely at the coming pages!

If you're feeling brave, turn the page to probe into the facts surrounding the human factory.

FULL OF HOT AIR

· · · · · · · · · · · · · ·

You probably already know that humans (like many other animals) produce gas. In fact, you can release up to 4 cups/1 liter of gas every day!

GAS GUZZLER

Some of the gas that comes in through your mouth needs to be released as a belch. There are various things that can cause you to swallow air:

loose dentures

fizzy drinks

swallowing air

chewing gum

smoking

PASSING WIND

The gases that aren't let out through your mouth pass through your digestive tract and are released through your anus.

BREAKING DOWN

Gases are created when food reaches your large intestine without having been digested by your small intestine first.

Bacteria in your body break down the food, creating gases in the process, including hydrogen, carbon dioxide, and, sometimes, methane—which is flammable!

CREATING A STINK

Some of these gases smell unpleasant and can make a noise as they are released out of your rectum as a fart.

BUILDING UP A SWEAT

Sweating is your body's way of keeping you cool.

COOL AS A CUCUMBER

Your body works like the inside of a fridge, carefully regulating its own temperature at about 98.6°F/37°C. When your body starts to overheat, you perspire, or sweat.

98.6°F/37°C

SENSITIVE MATTER

Sensors in your skin relay information to the hypothalamus in your brain, which sends a message back to your sweat glands.

YOU-TUBES

All over your body are small sweat glands, which are tiny tubes in your skin.

TIME TO CHILL

Your sweat glands respond to your brain's instructions and release perspiration to cool you down.

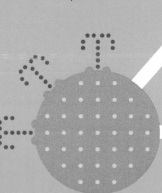

GETTING THE MESSAGE

Little holes in your skin called pores release this perspiration.

AIR CONDITIONED

As this perspiration hits the air, it evaporates off your skin, cooling you down.

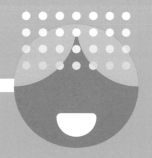

HUMAN HOTEL

The human body makes the perfect
place to stay for a number of creatures.

GUT BUSTER

Tapeworms can be
caught from eating
raw infected meat or
drinking contaminated
water. Most live in
your intestines and
can grow up to
50 feet/
15.2 meters long.

HOOKED UP

Hookworms are found
in the Americas, Africa,
and Asia and are
commonly caught by
walking barefoot on
infected ground. They
travel to your small
intestine and suck your
blood. They can go
undetected for years.

SCALP TAKER

Head lice live on your
head and attach their
eggs to your hair, close
to your scalp. Just one
female louse can lay
more than one hundred
eggs (known as nits) in
her forty-day lifetime.

TUNNEL VISION

Horseflies in Africa and
India can carry
Loa loa, also known as
eye worms, which grow
underneath your skin.
They bore holes
as they travel around
your body, eating
through layers of fat.

WORMING IN

A Guinea worm infection can be contracted by drinking contaminated water. The worm travels through your body and down a limb, where it emerges as a painful blister. Thanks to improved water supplies, this problem is increasingly rare in African countries where it was once common.

OUT ON A LIMB

Filarial worms are caught from infected mosquitoes in the tropics and subtropics. If they affect your lymph system, it can lead to a swelling of your limbs called elephantiasis, but you need to be bitten over many months before the effects take hold.

SWIMMING UPSTREAM

Candiru, or vampire fish, are tiny fish found in the Amazon Basin. There is a legend that they can swim up your urine stream into your urethra, although this is now proven to be a myth.

Ticks drive their feeding tubes through your skin to suck your blood. They are common around the world and can be picked up near livestock, in woods populated by deer, and in tropical climates.

PRODUCTION LINE

A veritable factory, the average human body contains and produces all kinds of substances! See what it has up its sleeve.

BIG BEARD

The Guinness Book of World Records has the longest beard at 17 feet, 6 inches/5.33 meters long.

BLOW OUT

With every sneeze, your nose releases around 40,000 droplets at up to 100 miles/160 kilometers per hour.

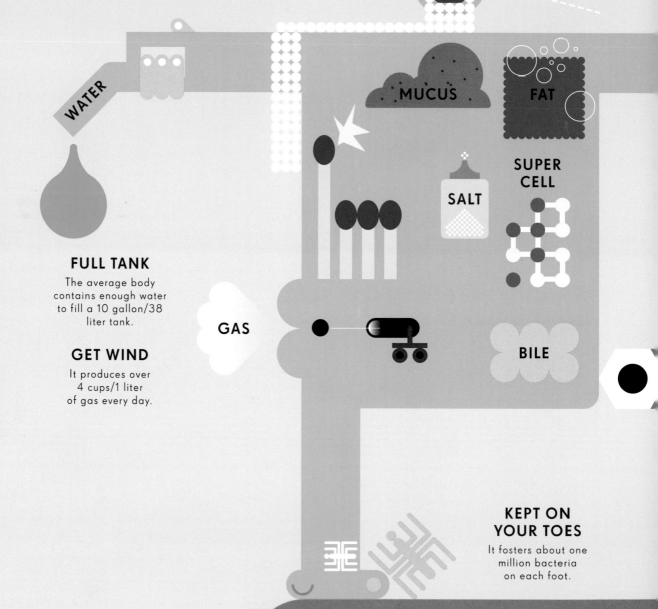

WATER

MUCUS

FAT

SALT

SUPER CELL

GAS

BILE

FULL TANK

The average body contains enough water to fill a 10 gallon/38 liter tank.

GET WIND

It produces over 4 cups/1 liter of gas every day.

KEPT ON YOUR TOES

It fosters about one million bacteria on each foot.

BOIL OVER

It gives off enough heat in thirty minutes to bring 3.4 pints/1.9 liters of water to a boil.

SOAP STORE

It contains enough fat to make up to seven bars of soap.

FLEA-BITTEN

It contains enough sulfur to kill all the fleas on an infested dog of average size.

PINCH OF SALT

It contains about 74 ounces/200 grams of sodium chloride, or salt.

SUPER CELL

It regenerates 300 million new cells every minute.

PENCIL PUSHER

It contains enough carbon to make up to 900 pencils.

DAY BILE DAY

It produces about 4 cups/1 liter of bile a day.

CARBON

CANNON FODDER

It contains enough potassium to fire a toy cannon.

FIRE STARTER

You can find enough phosphorus to make 2,200 match heads.

A LOT OF SNOT

It produces up to 4 cups/1 liter of mucus a day.

First U.S. edition 2014

Library of Congress Catalog Card Number pending
ISBN 978-0-7636-7123-5

13 14 15 16 17 18 CCP 10 9 8 7 6 5 4 3 2 1

Printed in Shenzhen, Guangdong, China

This book was typeset in Super Grotesk.
The illustrations were created digitally.

With thanks to Dr. Alec Broom and Ami Sedghi

BIG PICTURE PRESS
an imprint of
Candlewick Press
99 Dover Street
Somerville, Massachusetts 02144

www.candlewick.com
www.bigpicturepress.net

• •